Bleeding Rose

Priscilla Velez

BookLeaf Publishing

India | USA | UK

Presentation by *BookLeaf Publishing*

Web: www.bookleafpub.com

E-mail: info@bookleafpub.com

ISBN: 978-93-5744-921-2

First edition 2022

DEDICATION

To anyone that is carrying a heavy heart, I pray my words find you and resonate and uplift you.

ACKNOWLEDGEMENT

God.

My children for pushing me beyond my breaking points.

My mother for inspiring me through her own strengths.

My grandmother who has always been in my corner and has never let me down.

PREFACE

I'm sure we've all dealt with heartbreak or a break up before , well this is the story of the days following my recent heartache. I'm being completely vulnerable and raw, these poems are really like reading my diary.

Soul on Fire

We'll be nothing more than a memory
We've built nothing
but we're saying goodbye
what it could have been
I just fed me lies
Tears soak my pillow
stomach butterfly's

I try to stay strong
but I've been knocked
Where do I turn?
How can I stay?
I don't want us to fade

I beg of you
give me something comfortable to hold on
I'm losing me by holding onto you
Its pretty sick how much I deny it
I can't fake the funk

I'm losing it
losing you
losing me
all at once

Death is around the corner
but not up the street
there's someone digging to come out of me
I gotta love her
I gotta love her now
I should have loved her yesterday

Maybe
she would already be unbound

Who I am now
her heart is breaking
she yearns for someone
alive and still around

This silly girl with fantasy's
never ending happiness
how foolish can you be?

Silly girl
Heart on your sleeve
The man spoke truth
You did not hear you did not see
Only listened to speak

Now you choose to seek?
Silly girl must leave
transform

This chapter is ending
New life will rise
No more pretending
No more lies
from these ashes
roses will come alive

Let the waterfall
wash over you
let it dig into your wells
Drink the water that's clean with no smell

Soon You will drown
sink to the bottom of the ocean sea
Lose your breath
Ain't no controlling thee
Thou eateth of the fruit
That springs forth new life
You shall burn before you rise
So you might cherish the light.

Empty

You kiss my nose you kiss my head
Love on the brain
I want it dead
Can you even hear
or are you deaf
Can you not feel this
Cause I can feel this
I don't know if I can heal this
It hurts when I breathe
How do you deal
My eyes red and swollen
Brain ready to kill
Stomach turning
My soul is burning
Lifeless vessel
You've surpassed my threshold
Now you want me to let go
How when you're so special
Piece of heaven you gave me
I swear I could be having your baby
This whole thing is driving me crazy

Pitty

You're so close but so far
we almost made it
but almost means nothing if it falls apart
I just want the best for you
and the best for me
Such great company
I fed your soul while neglecting my own
I wanna love that lights up the sky
I thought it'd be you but I lied
I hate to say good bye
I never felt a love like this before
I think I'ma go cry

Do me a favor

Love me a little more on my bad days
Cause them sad days
can turn mad ways
some times I'm mad crazed
lost in a daze
thoughts running make me mad lazed
I'm sorry for my bad ways
I'm working on it
there's some things that get pushed up on it
I hate when we're opponents
I look up at the stars and wish upon it
better days when your loves up on me
I'm sorry but I just can't be phony
when I feel how I feel
man that shitis baloney
I just hate feeling lonely
just want you to hold me
console me
Tell me you won't let go me

You or Me

You'd rather lose me than choose me
Well fuck it then
I choose me
What's for me will be for me
No waiting no hoping no begging involved
I may love you but I love me too
If I'm not first I'm last
This is my life
so I'm in charge of the cast
I'm tired I'm over it
no more repeating the past
Feelings are hurt
hell yea I'm sad
What more do you want from me ?
It's driving me mad
Life's full of ups and downs
When's my turn to be glad?

Motions

When push comes to shove
ain't no telling the outcome
Yesterday I was better
today I'm slipping up some
My tarnished mind
don't know how to give you up
I'm trying to fill it with beauty
and things to pass time
but things from past times
are what keeps on coming up,
my memories a slave to you
the love feels so corrupt
I just wanna breathe you
when the sun is coming up
I go to bed without you
no more goodnights and love you's
Nothing to console
nothing to bring hope
Just trying to stay afloat
but I'm drowning on this boat
I lie so well I believe I'm over it
then come the stomach aches and I know this
thing ain't over kid.

Emotional roller coaster

Gotta focus on me
No more about us
I wanna settle sometimes
But I'm just losing my trust
I just wanna feel better
Been feeling under the weather
We supposed to be separating
So why are we still together
Hanging out everyday
ain't gonna make this no better
My love for you grows
Everytime you're around
I love when you're in town
But once you leave there's an ache
I know you feel it too
You're just some shit I can't shake
Someone pause the scene
Someone hit the brakes
I'm so in love with you
I have so much to say
That smile that face
That's why I tell you everyday

Every chance that I get
So if I ever lose you
I won't live with regret
I hope you know how much you mean to me
I hate it when you try to be mean to me
When You tell me you leaving
Makes it hard to breathe for me
Just wanna feel happy whole and love you free
fully.

What is love?

The controversy
That shows no mercy
Am I bestowed to be betrothed?
How does it feel? Can you feel it?
What do you hear when I speak it?
They say love is blind ,do you believe it?
Do you own me if I fall?
Will we be a union of souls
Something most can't comprehend
Love unconditional
Uncomfortable
Uncontrollable
Afraid and down right crazy
Oh my love you never cease to amaze me
Weather you raise me up or let me burn
I knew the stakes and chose to race
I am love , make no mistakes

To be honest

Im scared to be alone
I'm so out of my zone
I'm being told I don't need anything outside of
my soul
Everything that I think I can't be without
It's my own thoughts just speaking it out
I am whole and happy if I just make the choice
Allow myself to be a voice of reason
No more seasons of void
Lost souls become recognized souls
Do your part and let the truth unfold

Say it with your chest

Ima wait till it's real
no more time to kill
Sick and tired of being sick and tired
I just wanna heal
Don't bother hitting me up tryna chill
I'm busy getting my mind right
Outside the limelight
Can't wait till the times right
Gotta make it happen now
No more excuses
No more staying down
Tired of rolling around
Sipping with my friends all over town
Been on a roller coaster
still tryna hold my crown
I'm placing my feet on the ground
Standing tall
No more playing round

Somethings happening

Ashes to ashes
Dust to dust
Im really here
Being freed of lust
I was so confused
Having you was a must
I wasn't whole
You was always in a rush
I betrayed my own trust
I needed to be wanted
I didn't want me
I fed off of your attention
Affection
I indulged with greed

Then one day…

Memories no longer haunting
Breakthrough broke free
Loc'ed up my hair
Now I can see
Sunlight makes my eyes bright

I guess I stopped waiting
And made the time right

All this Beauty
All this peace
All that rage flew outta me
I'm amazed at who I see
My reflection staring back
And I repeat
This is me,this is me.

High off you

No shame in my pain
He has more to lose
But also more to gain
I don't feel any wrong so this gotta be right
Sweet emotions
Make me wanna hold you tight
I stand tall waiting through the night
Until the morning comes
And the sun shines it's light
I do not fear
For he holds me dear
I am not the one
To stay if the picture ain't clear
He's really seeing me now
And I know that he hears
My soul my cries
He can't help but be near
His arms around me
makes all the bad things disappear
He's so gentle but powerful
No wonder he's still here
The way you caress me
Stare
Nibble on my ear
You sway me to a place that I do not care

You love me
I love you
There's no need to look in your rear

Over thinking

It took less than a day
For you to show me once again
Why I can't be here
I'm reiterating myself
Speaking boundaries
You cross them so easily
You know it pains me
To be here
Why do you do this?
Lift me up
Then throw me away
I can't take it anymore
You don't deserve my tears
You know exactly what you're doing
Stop playing with me
Stop fucking playing with me
You always get your way
I'm so fucking tired of this
Bullshit
All of that ends today
Now I'm angry
You're pulling me down
By staying around
I need to keep my peace
Once you go

I may frown
But I promise you
Nah fuck that
I promise me
I'm gonna stand my ground

Sorry again

Well I guess I overreacted
My bad
I hate when that happens
My emotions sometimes make me reactive
I try and control them
Hopefully you can manage
Thankfully
You didn't even know
How I was laid up in my bed
Cussing you out inside my head
This bonding shit is crazy
Makes me think all types of shit
Makes me a little hazy
I'm in a weird place right now
Mentally
I feel like I'm getting on track
Then I get sucked back into our melody
Maybe it's meant to be
I sure hope it is
And if it's not
this lesson is the remedy
For life long changes in my identity
You made me smile this morning
Morning sunshine
Is what you said to me

I'm really lost in your entity
I need to bring it down a notch
Maybe two or three
Can't lie I just wanna be done with me
I be throwing shots like loose cannons
I keep it inside though
You know my ass is always on go
But I'm trying not to stress you out
So I can't let you know

In my feelings

Why is it that your love comes with conditions?
If I was to act up you'd be gone
I gotta stay in line
I gotta listen
If I wanna have any type of commitment
I choose to keep you happy
I be wondering why though
Losing anyone outside myself ain't an issue
Trust I be knowing better
Just not choosing better
I'm quite far from nieve
It's just this damn heart on my sleeve
Shit be killing me
Let men be my weakness
The attention and love
All that sweet shit
I just eat it up
But I'm not no weak bitch
Just when it comes to you
I don't know
Thinking of not having you makes me sick
Fatigued
Like I'm sailing on a ship
I'm ready to crash
Ready to burn

Abandon all this
I don't need conditional love
I need the type that stays regardless

Conflicted

He's trying to flip the script now
I see shit flying a mile away
Nobody wants to be the bad guy
But we're not about to just sit around and play
Manipulation
I've been through that a million types of ways
I'll be fucking damned if I deal with that today
See your actions and words ain't matching
Spare me the excuse
You're only going to cause a reaction
Thinking im a buy your transaction
I ain't the one to be with all the cappin
I'm a tell you how I feel
Once the convo starts clappin
We having an honest conversation?
Don't be cautious
Lay it bare
Talk to me
Let me hear
Now Listen to me
Do you even care?
I guess not
My mind is too complex
You don't understand half the shit I tell you

I could cry in your face
As I have many times
You still be lost wondering why
Your assumptions be so far off
Annoys the shit out of me
I thought you'd understand
I'm firm in who I am
But at times I feel I'm damned
I guess loving you is wrong
You got my mind so fucking crammed

Inner child

I'm pretty sure I'm breaking
Maybe repairing
I'm not sure
I know I'm getting antsy
Somethings gotta give
I'm getting angry
I know what I deserve
Why isn't he giving me it
Got me questioning my worth
Hell no
We ain't doing that
We've worked too hard
To get where we are
Mentally
Physically
You can't even see the scars
Me and my younger self
We used to always feel subpar
But fuck all that noise
Now we raising the bar
Standards
Yea them things are still flawed
But We're aware
No more choosing those that don't choose us
Only picking those that take us far

21 days to break a
habit

It's been 3 weeks since we claimed we're over
Can't lie it's been hard
It's been real
Went soul searching
Just trying to deal
Heal
I looked deep
So deep
I got new beliefs
New perspectives
Most couldn't comprehend this
In the process of losing you
I learned a lesson
I gotta remember that this life is a blessing
No more settling
Putting myself through transgressions
In the name of love
I choose me
Today
Tomorrow
Every week
I know this has been one hell of a ride

But now you see the way I stride
This is how I survive
I crash and burn
Then come back alive
Stronger than ever
I can handle any weather
Rain
Snow
Heat
There ain't nothing I can't beat
I'm a vulnerable woman
That is my power
To love and to hold
No matter the showers
One day the right one will find me
But I'm not counting the hours
Till then
me and my younger self will just be ours